T0114949

BIRTHCRY

POEMS

Kraftgriots

Also in the series (POETRY)

BIRTHCRY

◇ ◇ ◇ ◇ ◇ ◇ ◇

POEMS

Obi Nwakanma

kraftgriots

Published by
Kraft Books Limited
6A Polytechnic Road, Sango, Ibadan
Box 22084, University of Ibadan Post Office
Ibadan, Oyo State, Nigeria
℘ +234 (0)803 348 2474, +234 (0)805 129 1191
E-mail: kraftbooks@yahoo.com;
kraftbookslimited@gmail.com
Website: www.kraftbookslimited.com

First published 2016

ISBN 978–978–918–368–5

= KRAFTGRIOTS =
(A literary imprint of Kraft Books Limited)

First printing, March 2016

For Kiran Amaechina Dikeocha
May your lineage never end

ACKNOWLEDGMENTS

The poems in this collection emerged out of the experience of a new life—both in terms of a displacement from an old, familiar place, to a new one, and in terms of welcoming a child to the world. In both cases, the experience is communal. I would like thus to thank all of the people who have shared with me the experience of *Birthcry*. I am grateful to Washington University in St. Louis, whose generous grant allowed me contemplation. To the poets, Carl Phillips and Mary Jo Bang, from whom I've learned the power of precise images, I say thank you. And most importantly, I wish to acknowledge and thank my wife Mira, muse and critic at once, in whose careful fingers most of these poems have turned, from dough to leavened bread.

CONTENTS

THE STORY IS A DONKEY

Child –

The story is a donkey,
Carrying the burden of the age.
The swift gazelle may outrun the wilderness,
But never the light.

The story is a harlot too,
Serving her numerous masters
Who pay in hard currency,
Or win her by lot, in the game of numbers.

ORPHEUS DESCENDING

Your steps, through the lunar cycle
Draw you homeward, child.
You hear, you hear the sounds
Of this world: the rattling panes
Of glass, and from the wind, the rush
Of stirred waters.

The child longs for home,
Restless in the womb,
Listening to the wail of the violin,
To the beckoning of a Bach sonata.

Through the voices echoing homeward,
And magnified in the maternal fluid—
The primal sea of creation—
You hear, you hear the breathless morning.

AT SHORE, WITH THE STARS

We are both storytellers:
You, of what is to become,
and I, of what has gone before.
Certitude sometimes returns as faith,
as the image of the stars.

This night as I muse your coming,
counting the named constellations,
crossing the imaginary lines where stars cluster,
I know that what has changed
is the way we read the night.

Not the narratives
tracing an invented people.
Not the black emptiness
that surrounds us.

FOR FIDA

Born February 25, 2002, Nablus

There, in the cool of morning,
Out of the mist of the future,
Out of the rumours floating from the seas
Of Arabia –
Out of a fragrant time,
Came my moon-wreathed companion,
Traveling through flood-lit night,
Her cries are hard, like a wretched stare.

Before curfew unwound
From the throat of the rooster,
Came my stricken companion,
With child –
From the perpetual stillness of that night,
When the lone light from a lamp
Moved from threshold to threshold,
Looking for peace and a manger.

FLUTE FOR HANDMAIDENS

March is for handmaidens
   – those wrought in the equinox:

Those who walked whole market weeks,
Trading with the full moon,
Who led the march,
Clenching in dissent,
The fist of the homeland,
Like the women of Chiapas,
Like the Aba matriarchs,
In the lineage of Nwanyieke Amu[1] –
These, whose wombs gave birth to miracles:

>Da Agne –
>Da Louisa –
>Da Kati –
>Da Berna –
>Da Ange –

Mothers of my lineage.
They invite you, goddess,
From the alien temples of Shiva
To join the moondance;
To become – Mirabai –
One with your dark one.

---

[1]   My great grandmother, also known in the colonial reports as Nwanyieke Ahiara, who led the women to Ahiara in the famous women's uprising against colonialism in 1929.

THE HARSH WIND ORCHESTRA

The harsh wind orchestra

Played in the hidden corner of night.

Each star,

Exhausted now by carousing,

Ascended the spiraling tower,

Towards Babylon,

To the crack of bitter voices.

And there,

They die of free love.

In the Mid-noon of our Lives

In the mid-noon of our lives
We dragged our burlap bags
Across highways.
We carried the fog in our souls
And the clouds high, above our heads.
We smelled the sun-soaked grass
And the afternoon rain.
We glimpsed a sunrise, and knew it,
Before it vanished from sight;
And of the quicksand,
This uncertain depth concealed it.
Of the world and its sufficient causes,
There are too many centuries between us.
The sun hurries down beyond the ridges.
The liquid rays rush recklessly alongside,
Rousing the ageless storm. Fear slips between
Like a careless word in a sentence.

THE WAYFARER'S SONG

We kept our tears fostered in the gourd,
In the Cafora, over Arab coffee,
And gingerbread, in the floating nights,
And the hot voices arguing above the Atlantic,
The spent night still yields – lachrymae –

To the dead of Gaza –
The eyeless rites of the fire circle

Singing:
"May we live long enough
through these bruised years,
May we escape our tears,
And our fears of the night,
From this rage…this rage …
From this prison that is the body,
From the womb that holds us, stilled."

On the Cusp of the Day

These are my memoirs
Of a day, not blunted, not dispersed
Or vulnerable, not manacled
By restraining orders, and interim injunctions.

The shuttle to the sea, the shuttle
To dawn, is full of design: deliberate,
Like an ordained view,
In a world fully conscious of itself.

It speaks about your arrival, child,
And like all ordained things,
The ninth month awaits you.

BIRTHCRY

There is a place for the kindred.
And we gathered – this memorial week –
To celebrate wine. Did you see, with your
Foetal eyes, how the cloud lifted, revealing the sun,
Each time the face of the earth darkened
With tears?

Did you, from the portals of the unborn,
Hear the many footsteps
Those who have gone before you
The birthcries, inviolate moments,
On the lips of mornings?

Faith, daughter of the world
Seeking a place among her own;
And Khadija, jewel of Casa Blanca,
Coming out of her mourning –

The birthcries are the same.
The first is all –
Is always the beginning

Of the pristine journey to life.
Without a kink.

Infinite.

SATURDAY MORNING

By noon, we finished painting the cosmos,
And washing the dry paints from our fingers.
We arranged the table for coffee,
And filled the flowervase.

We re-enact our abilities partly as triumph,
Partly as a sequence of delayed accidents,
Partly to covet the women with whom we are interpolated,
Partly to halt the nightmare of a meaningless life,
And partly to mutter the drunken truth:
¡No se puede vivir sin amor![2]

---

[2]   Without love, it's not possible to live!

MIRABAI, MIRABAI –

The birthroom awaits you,
The birthpangs will clench you,
The midwife will hold you –
But where is the labour most wont?
There in the ghost town?
In Places for people? There –
Walking quietly among the wounded,
Among the hungry, handing to them
A jug of wine, here, a cup of coffee, there,
A gourd of charity. Here where thirst is affliction,
She is their countess, queen of their hearts.

Where they live their lives
On crutches
And countless ironies
And estrangements.
Where they live their lives diagonally
On luminous loves,
Despite the polished pebbles
From sea to sea
Upward-downward the roman à clef,
Where thirst is affliction,
Where labour is most wont.

A CONVERSION

We await the child,
Like the dark cygnets the night
Gliding by, the ripples,
The falling light and autumnal leaves
Floating wingless
In the afternoon.
Let the gods buried inside us
Free themselves, become reborn
And human again,
For each new birth is the call of the muezzin
Rousing us to a new faith.

ORPHEUS AT THE GATES

i.

O child!

I have gathered epiphanies like religion,
Surveying each sketched autobiography,
The marquee of narrative bodies,
The hierophantic inscription, like a Mayan sign.

I have chosen a date for your arrival.
I have built a crib from a constellation
Of love letters.
I have given you a name.

ii.

There is a period of absorption, and
    Of oblivion –
A time to chant with the maracas
    And toast with the frosty beer –
A time to show the sparkle on my patent leather shoes –
    To dance once again with the houris of Ayilara.

iii.

This intoxication, I told myself, is like
Approaching the death of speech. A stirring
That stupefies thirst. The lyrical nature
Of joy is like an infant's first smile.
That neon arc that shapes the world.

In the Steps of Manuel Sendero

At dusk, a woman leaned into the earth
To clutch a child.

The one is smooth as butter,
And the mother: O Madonna –
The stars are in her eyes.

> The road is flint –
> > The road is flint –
> > > And to those who follow –
> > > > It is the place of legend:

Of the child who refused to come
On the anointed day:

A glimpse of the threshold startled him!
The running waters rattled him!
The loud arguments of war frightened him!

The soldier ants have clawed their way through the womb
To wrest the unborn, his limb, his will,
But the eternal doorway remains barred –

> The road is flint:
> It is the place of metaphor.

LIBATION

Child – root of the Iroko – descend
Slowly, hold tautly to the stake of life,
Do not run like the seasonal flood,
Rushing away, homeless.

AMONG THE STONES

i.

We feel among the stones
For new growths,
For the remains of the day:
But the old are passing in their numbers,
The past is coming home to us.
A holly-hock raised her skinny stem
In protest against passing time.

The breviary, the place of unction,
Somehow revives the prostrate dream
Of a new breed to people the earth.
We awake in the region of that dream,
Desolate, fountains of water returning
Home to their source.

We have allowed our souls
To wander, remorselessly over time.
Over the burning sea.
The potent meditative flow.
The juice and the jouissance.
The compelling fiction
Of theories, its arc of the haunted
Edgy, redemptive self.

The child in the rest of us, glowing,
Willing, trembling to be born,
Straining after the moon in its fullest,
Behind the curtain, over folds,
Over folds of deepest night, loosens
The castrate tongue.

ii.

It must be that mystic hour –
The time of all awakening, of all birth,
Of the quickening of the womb.
It must be a time of discovery
About mortality, mutability.

Child: you will see strength in my face,
The first time your eyes open,
You may see glorious history,
Or its illegitimacy: but I
Will be more than those histories.

I will be a sojourner from a tangled past
Traveling to an uncertain future.
I will be history broken into many tremulous things.
I will be the twin threshold of time, the many rivers
That have flowed in it, and the many suns
That have risen over the hills.
I will be the road, and its unquenchable thirst.

RECITING ELIZABETH BISHOP OVER MORNING TEA

The fierce wintry gale lifted the skirts of heaven,
And allowed the menstrual blood
To flow. Since history
Is about movement, it flowed –
And flowed – until the blood became the sea.

Winter became spring. The hand of the offspring of storms
Fluttered. The womb kept her guest warmed by the fireplace.
The hand of the seasonal clock struck against cobwebs.
Dusted, the hacienda, the villa of life waited
To open its gates to resplendent spring. Winter became spring.

And soon in the bulge, like the slow rising of leavened bread,
A hand brushed against the nightairs.
It stirred, bird like, roiling, as the waves of Bar Harbor,
Like the hard dark tears that boil on the stove
For morning tea, the prenatal chamomile.

Winter became spring, and grew the fur and hooves
Of some night animal. For pastime, drinking sherry and hot grogs
With the innkeeper's moll, whispering Miss Bishop to the unborn,
And to the hot tears that boil on the prenatal stove, at the harbour,
After codfish and chowder, and Miss Bishop:

>	*Do ye bile yer kettle out?*

A journey in the belly of night
Will bring us to the shore, to Nineveh,
To the little carousel,
Before we took fright from the broken water,
At the harbour, O Miss Bishop:

>	*Do ye bile yer kettle out?*

Do you even know how we were altered by spring,
As she turned her face from winter, away from the portals
Of a dead time, from infertility, towards fruition?
Should we boil the kettle then? Should we call the ambulance?
Should we wait at the door, and listen to the first birthpangs?

INGRESS

The bare pubes refreshed,
The womb is slow in quickening.
The tendril forms, the body before the morning,
Comes to the paternal gaze.

It is the ornate bottle with liquid densities,
It is the cup overflowing with viscera,
It is the cupola and minaret of desires,
It is the envelope with a letter to the future,
It is the dawn with its yellowing light,
It is the opaque and fragile ways of innocence.

ERI NA AMAKU

From the myth of Eos and Orion

i.

The minutes unwound with the cries rocking the chamber.
The mother's body suffered for release.
There was a different expanse, a different language between us.
The anaesthetic plunged back into the polished time.

And this is my greatest fear: the threat of being identical.
I am a swimmer into phantom: four laps behind the sun,
I arrive at an endless river. At its shores, the water is invisible
It flows in time, in the cadence of wind and fire: and then,

The opaque red tinkling into the jar.
On the small cart, the crucifix –
A nail embedded into its skull –
Hangs in fierce boredom,
Staring down at childbirth. Sanctioning.

ii.

My own hands bathed the clitoral lips of a lover
And unsealed the silence from that entry into the world.

Sometimes, because I have erred and offered casual caress,
My hinges opened to the dark street.
Sometimes because I resist interpretation, because
Pilgrims arrive daily amidst wilted nights and mutating stars,
Sometimes because of the insatiable cadence,
The meaningless repetitions become acts of grace.
I become the caress, repetitive, casual.

iii.

This night is not casual –
It is insatiable and full of rain,
The wind is dancing on the streets.

The broken water, like the surge of rivulets,
Announces a time, which will harden into myth.
The stars drift. The stars gather
At the belt of Orion. Northwards.
In celestial buntings.

iv.

So the old fables lead to the rock –
Where we must bury your umbilical cord.
To the night, in which you and I
Crossed the lifeline, and bonded.

You, dripping with primeval blood,
Your eyes, the depth of the sea,
Claiming everything around it.
And to that night –

In the elegant company of the stars,
You came riding with the storm, in the pose
Of the ancients, guardians of the tribe,
Clasping the wind to your bosom.

Le Petit Mort

He thought it was death upon him,
To be displayed for all to see.
He hurried towards the crowded room,
White cloaks, wailing, and a sigh.
It was the time of judgment.
He arrived into his own name.

His genitals are perfectly formed.
He has ten fingers, ten toes.
I hold the silk of his skin,
Peering into the gossamer clarity of a body,
Through which flows my blood, like lava,
Like seasoned wine in a new cask.

KNOTS OF A RUFFIAN WIND

The faces returned to me at 2 o'clock.
The ones that I had forgotten – watery –
The rush of memory filled my blood
With juice. I stood then with time erect
Like an active organ on duty, unflagging,
Riding the horses of memory. I remembered
Biafra – another birth stirred by time –stilled
The ancestral cry breached by holocaust –
On the shinning path, and in the light
Of the winged serpent of the sky, welcomes
The new one. Every seed, every twitch of light
Contains history. And so do you, my child.

THE TRAVELER

The traveler from another world, at the signal
from the blistered sky, dismounted.
And he came and shook off nine months of dust
And stretched his limbs and uttered a cry.

Light seeps through the cloister of blood, light
and the cord that earths the seed,
feeds the sapling
with the power of love.

SEASON OF FORGETTING

I have been to Bujumbura –
And I have seen the carnage.
I have seen the trees dripping with bitter tears
Each milestone marked with blood.
I have seen the hills go blind
With memory.
There, where their eyes saw
A tideswell, and fury unburdened
Like a deformed child from its womb.
I have seen Kigali grow dry in the sun,
I have seen Kigali, beautiful maiden
Of the great lakes, now lying among the
Raped, south of the cape of good hope.

But child,
Why have you chosen, of the many seasons,
This to be born?

We look to the stars for signs.
We plead with celestial distance.
The strains that play in the night, child,
At the peak of the season, are the same.
Clatter of the hooves of war,
On the streets.
I have heard these strains before,
I have seen fire billow out of the crypt
In the many names of God. Out of the voice
Of the anvil – the hood of Pomponazzi –
The dogma of the three laws, the shape of the hands
Of the beast, the cruel time that is
Upon us. I have seen it all.

But why, I ask -
Of all seasons,
Have you chosen this to come?

THE MEASURE OF THINGS

I have measured you in my hands:
What you weigh is my future.
It is the burden which you share.
Your life is in two spans:
The time of growth,
And the time of death.

But of all these –
Death astounds infinitely.
Life springs out of the plough.
It is the murmuring river:
We race towards it,
Because it is familiar.

It is the breadth of something
More infinite than thirst.
The little life in a cot, trembling with sleep,
Is the past, and the future,
And the continuous present.
It is immortality wrapped in a bundle.

VOYAGER

And now,
On a cloudy Sunday,
A child lies naked before me.

How you have slumbered through the ages,
And awakened with rain.

If carnivore spirits may only look at your face,
The repose, the calm wind of your life,
Should still the tumult in the land.

Black Sunday

For the thousand victims of an explosion at the Ikeja arms depot
January 27, 2002, Lagos

The god who answereth by fire descended
On this day, and joined the Christians
In their holy rites — possessed, in celebration,
Sweating sin through the pores of midnoon.

Long invoked, in ceaseless passion,
In tongues stiffened by prophecy,
Loosened by pentecost,
In the fire rites to Beelzebub

He blazed through the feathered circuit,
Potent –
He came disguised as a child
And entered the camp of warriors.

TWENTY-NINE STEPS

It may be a sign, when you grapple
The umbilical cord – the power that earths you
To the womb. Child, the cycle of blood
Overwhelms me: Today, we celebrate with laden breath,
Twenty-nine steps from the land of spirits.
Your approach through windswept night,
Through the ancient corridor,
Is a chronology that fills me with dread.

It is the dance of the earth that frightens me.
It is Petah Tikvah today. The scar remains still
On the soul. A child was burnt in the inferno.
Her scream cannot be buried in a grave.
And I have carried in my weary ears,
The cries of those who lie in unmarked graves.
The voice of death carries a long forgotten truth:
"The future is the charred remains of another day."

In Nablus – in the camp of discontent –
There is only horror in the eyes of a mother,
As the wind, swollen by these vivid moments,
Explodes into a chant.

In memory, Leonard Gakinya

Found Hanged October 2, 2002, in Springfield, Missouri

And I remember the gnat
And the tribe of singing leaves.
And I remember the imperial leaf
Bent finally to the sun.

Dark, brooding –
The face of a fallen saint
Upon him; angry –
Bole of giant maleness
Roiling impotently through poetry.

He impaled every noon
With a dark erect malevolence, and like
The gay adder strikes
Where the grass is greenest.

And I remember the smouldering hearth, the bitch in heat –
The unsurveyed pudenda – the unvisited hacienda
Echoing to itself, ventriloquizing the wind.
Melanin is under my skin, and that is nothing new either.
But let me tell it…let me tell it all …

Of the one night when the moon sank
Under my skin. And I made love to Prozac,
To ecstasy, and sang the ode to forgetting,
Toasting midnight with Bella Sera beside me.
But let me tell it…let me tell it all …

Of the deaf blue sky,

On the day I rose, and raised
My hand for more wine,
And raised my glass –
To morning's nipples hardening
                    Before me.

To the god who created pain as he created wine
To the adze waiting to shape the wood
To the nights variable and uncertain
To my shadow standing, hands akimbo,
Across twenty yards
To the terraces of comely St. Louis –

Let me tell it…let me tell it all…
(for melanin is under my skin)

Of the sea of snarling faces on Delmar, pale,
Angry, staggering against the light,
And the night who offered herself to me
As temptation: to jump and hang
From a ten-storied sky –
The gossamer rope lowering the body
To enlightenment,
From the seventh ether to the ninth symphony, and then
The final footfall, and Beethoven belching
From the solemn dirge –

Let me tell it all, child, let me tell –

Of the chthonic place, the hall of fame,
And how it hurts so. For I remember the gnat,
Stuck on the scrotum, sacerdotal,
With the intangible –
The undiagnosed disorder –
The obsessed, importunate and wonderful

Lie that suffers the self, and nails
To the cross – all desires –
To be plain. To be a child.
To cross the body, and its soul
And to say: "amen."

A Time to Gather

i.

There is a time to gather
     and a time to be gathered –
To stretch the arm and become a wing,
     to be the hen, sheltering her brood from the rain.

There is a time for rain,
     its purifying strain on the roof –
A time to fly
     to the embrace of sleep.

There is a time to sleep and to wake
     with an infant in the light –
To be the light and the infant once again,
     roused slowly out of barren time.

A time to walk, to take the first uncertain steps
     and a time to run, to return to a sheltering place –
To be the elegant moon
     Striding home wistfully.

ii.

There is a time to be full and adequate
        and a time to be minimal –
Like the miniskirt
        holding joys intangibly.

To be the half-revealed
        the stilled waters –
In the place where inlets
        yield echoes from stones.

There is the time of the stone –
And time of the builder with stones.

MY TONGUE WAS LANDLOCKED

My tongue was landlocked.
It has been freed by new life.
I have lived in lapses, and sometimes,
In lucid dreams. Like the kernel
In the flesh of the fruit –
I have lived in aeons of abstraction,
In comfort zones and bath-houses.

I have jumped queues in pursuit
Of the horizons. Like the stars –
I have straddled horizons. And yet,
The firefly thinks itself a star, and dives
Into anonymity. It must be the new life
That has freed me,
From a time lived in lapses and in abstraction.

A Brief Memoir of Time

King Leopold sent an
emissary. The English
Realm sent a viceroy.
The Americans had a
Trade mission. The picture
was complete. The
Rising of the sun came.
The horse-drawn carriage,
Bearing the royal insignia,
came cantering on
The cobblestones.
There was no Hamlet.
It was only
The rumpled figure of the
Prince of Belgium. His eyes,
The colour of whiskey,
held the archives of midnight's
Carousing. The colonnades,
the great imperial statues,
The imported battalion, standing mutely
outside the street,
Saluted his royal highness.

His mind was still cluttered
With sleep, the virginal fluids
of a raped continent, fresh in his
Waking, still coursed in his veins.
He rehearsed the royal proclamation,
the post-colonial dicta,
carefully in his thoughts;
And he mounted the rostrum,

and uttered his farewell,
And smiled into the microphone,
and shook his gloved hands
With the natives, and sat heavily,
like the guest of honour,
to courteous silence:

He could not bear it –
Lumumba could not bear it,

He rose, and spoke
about the pain of the true Congo,
Which U Tam'si, poet of the pagan soul,
had sung hoarsely about,
His voice broken, he died in exile,
still mourning the bloody river.

He could not bear it –
Lumumba could not bear it –

He shook his hands in the face of the prince,
He raged, and raged, and raged like the storm,
He tore his hair, and rolled his sleeves,
And dared the prince of Belgium
to a wrestling match.

O, Lumumba –
They shaved his head and blinded his eyes,
They whipped him with hide
and put him to the sword.
They flayed his acolytes, and in death, fed them
To the swine. The remnant, those saved
By the silent veil, fled to the hills.

Child, you will remember him, Lumumba,
With your vegetable offering,
At the festival of the ancestors.

And what do we say of Mandela?
Age alone, fostered him to tell
The tale of the century.
There is a place on Robben Island,
Where he was sent to contemplate his
Transgressions. Where we found him
breaking stones,
Counting from the sky's
sodden parchment,

How many seasons
that the moon had crossed,
How many slivers of rain,
like those stones,
Could make a flood.

And Sisulu with him, read
His eyes blind with Das Kapital.
As each tooth
Fell from their gums,
they knew deep in their hearts,
That time was fleeing from them.

We may be in the grip of the cobweb once more
But we are unbruised by fear, my child.
I will tell you,
That you may be of good cheer,
that you may remember,
That war and pestilence have graced our heels.
But from our land
have sprouted sturdy boles of the Iroko,
watered by tears.
We have grown mute
to the howl of scud missiles,
For they fall like ripened pears
at the feet of children.

We have lived the years
of the cannibal rage, and so,
To whom do we make our plea?

They say we must
Cast a spell on the future;
that we must pluck the future
Before its ripening,
with new age theories, strange
Economic broth,
the consensus of the obliged.

I say,
Child, may our twilights cross
the bow of predatory snares.

THE WORD IS OUR MEMORY

As you know, Mirabai,
The word is the memory of the race.
But what shall I do with these images
That nurture my lust?

The power that crosses the Red Sea
Flees with the arrows of the rain,
They put a yoke on the tribe, and
A curfew, like shackles, on the evening.
The beast whose lair is in the hills
Roams unwearied from year to year.
And so I see, and shape my voice of the stranger,
And borrow from this alien tongue, the words
To soothe the lusts that nurture me.

THE EAGLE AND THE IROKO

O Child –
The Eagle that perches on an Iroko,
Has found a fitting place to rest.
So, I anoint you before greatness.

The eyes that see great deeds,
Will itself be full.
Like the ripening of the corn,
Let your eyes be full.

Let the wings of the eagle
Stretch –
And the days of the child
From season unto season.

NIGHT

We are kindling the flames –
And for reason –
To blend sensibility with tallow.

The candle burns off decorated fire,
The pomander, the scents of life,
And you have yielded through satin
As the centuries through ages –

And every night is still shaped
By the stars –
By your cries.

A MANNER OF SPEECH

Mirabai, Mirabai –
mother of the child,
and of the devout verse:
Freedom is a manner of speech,
And "misspelling is a form
Of sorcery."

I can now sit and sift through the grey
Pictures. The frayed edges, pastured,
Silken mist, deep as a lake
Of clear water, and a mirror
Containing, not a ghost,
Not an irregular and nervous view,
Not a contained, unequal, a spent view.

I can sit now and hear the stampede. Oracular.
Where mountains are invoked, and they become
Glaciers. A village square. A little spot
Near Vaughn Street. Spectroscopic. And simple –
The dandelion – the towncrying cockerel,
The sign of whom is,
The white, indissoluble sky.

Mirabai, Mirabai –
Freedom is a manner of speech:

And my story is of night's darkening face,
And they who feed of it.
Those who will mount the steeples,
Following an ascent, until ascent becomes descent,
Becomes meaningless: becomes the elegy of belltowers,
At the death of a dream. I hear even now,
The stampede, the story of the herd,
Fleeing from the homeland.

COMMUNION

I am the master of poetic sarcasm — the balladeer —
And what do I know of the dialogue
Between the mortar and pestle?
Only this:
That between them, they grind
The wheat into flour
The flour becomes bread
And the bread becomes
The body of Christ
And Christ always dies on the cross.

What They Left Us

Aksum lies forlorn in the East,
Zambezi, her mouth shriveled
Like the dried yellow corn
For the next planting season.

The Limpopo –
Supine, lethargic.

The innards of the Congo
Bruised by the strange thrusts of spears,
From Stanley to Mobutu,
And their legacy of bones.

Passover

Then we stopped for a drink of pure dew
Near the stream of Eri, before the pass to Agukwu –
With alabaster mugs, drank of the juice
From the breast of the earth –
Where the breathless, ungodly hour
Wrapped its furs around us.

In fours, quadrilineal, are the laws
Of the great beast, child,
The mark of whom is on my breath.
Strange is that alien tongue that names me.
The rites led us through the gates.
The season of the counting was upon us.

We return, in the festival of the ancestors,
Always with our offerings
Of vegetables & yam, and wine
And fat young ewes –
With hooded eyes, our heads bowed
Shorn of hair and memory.

A STIRRING

These dark stirrings are consolations,
Which tenderly, almost without fear,
Like epic labour,
Like clairvoyance, possess me,
Like a lyric,
Dantesque:

There is purpose, O child, who has sprouted,
Like a dream, each drachma, the weight in gold.

There is lineage to your name,
There have been tauter nights
When we mingled with history,
There have been spigots
Which have turned into ingots.

There is in your stirring, O child, a story –
The tassels of robed seasons.

MARCH 15

O wind that bends the strongest boles
The goat that does not chew on stones –
       Wererese![3]
If the seasons ripen, pray, pluck one
For the wanderer –
       Wererese!
If the seasons do not ripen, pray, pluck same
For the sojourner –
       Wererese!

Flight of the white bird, O she
Who shapes the form of the bough,
Remember, there is nemesis for the hand
That yokes the bow to the arrow.

I saw the falcons
On the rise of five suns,
They flew inclined
Towards the East.

And in the crash of tameless waves against
The rocks at rock harbour, I saw the pelican-mother,
Weaning her child on mandrake, and the juice
Of her vein, that he may suckle and grow fierce.

O wind that bows the greatest boles –
If the harvest comes –
       Wererese!
Pray shake the fruits
From the hands of the branches.
       Wererese!

---

[3]   An Igbo exclamation used during call and response.

A Touch of Scarlet

A touch of scarlet in the green river
To make the blind see
A flash of contrasts before one's
Eyes. Then the decor becomes monotonous.

Pale faces, no shade of darkness, the same green
Veins stretching to the sun; the hurrying
Steps like the receding sea
Pointless – homeless – just the rush
Of a mad conformity.

The night is rich with copper. There, in the
Chill of heavy wind, the dug-out is moored,
To ferry Lumumba across the waves, but the night
Lies in wait for the passing of the stars.

It is the same road that Mpolo took, Okito behind,
The revolution engineered with the accompaniments
Of borrowed guns. But who says the wind does not hear
Words spoken in secret? Who says the wind can be trapped
In snares wider than time?

SEED

We are no longer the gods of certitude.
All sounds come from under the water –
All sounds are the sea. Obscure.

We are not the gods riding breathlessly
Towards anonymity –
And I speak simply of a furled leaf,

Unfurling. Not the drifter drifting
Towards the black hole, but back
Into the narrative space that contains a wry, organic world.

There, in the radiant void,
Lives the shadow of all things
That pervades the changing world.

We are no longer the gods of antiquity.
The image of a dark, unforgiving night,
Whose interior shadow haunts.

We are the word spoken to the tribe.
Not the severe, minimalist monologue,
Not the barren womb, which contains no child.

Missa Solemnis

For Bola Ige

In death, they say, there is neither
right nor wrong:
we must as evemist to the grass
anoint the dead,
seal the wound,
put balm
where the hot blade pierces the heart.

Night is a mask, is the mollusk,
yielding its flesh; the fierce,
the vivid whisper, flooding the plain.
And then, the cock that mounts the stonewall,
stretches his throat,
and announces the ingathering,
and the fragrance of rain.

And what shall we do
with the needless, wordless
rhyme,
of lives filled with significance?
What accurate, intimate thing
shall be a monument,
like the surface of the coral reef?

The tongue, licking its answer,
blurs, further blurs, the telling.
For we still dare to dream
about fragility,
about how – intertwined with disguise –
it is essence:
how each petal still hangs loosely on the branch.

WE LEARN TO LIVE IN SIMPLE WAYS

We learn to live in simple ways
With the angle of sleep that makes a child's face tender
In the quaint domesticities of waking to nightly stirrings
To the uncertainty of rising
When none is sure that the infant's sleep
is not the final one.
Before the spirit takes form
And escapes through the last breath
Or through the pore of night.

We learn to live in ordinary ways
To drink socially, and appear novel
To hold the phone in a long galactic dialogue
To count the smooth dents that we make with each footfall
And find a spot somewhere between the waver of doubt.

We learn to fall deeply in love again
To say bright words
To stop counting the bodies in war
To stand in the light
Fit the gables in a new house
Read the Boston Globe
And chat on krazitivity.

BENEDICTION

In time, your room will be adolescent.
And I will lose you to music
Or to new age religion.
But let me now bless your gestures, child,
As your fingers clutch, fevered, to mine.
Let us feel this primal heat
Until we begin our struggle
For the same womb, seed of my loins:
I have glimpsed eternity in your eyes.
I have also seen the future.
But I am driven by fear
As with love
To shield you from it.

CHILD OF FOUR WINDS

i.

In the mill city came the voice
Of the indigo peasants calling the son of the grocer
To Shihar, to teach them the peace of cottonfields –
Among them, those for whom the wheel turns, enlightened,
For drawn on the seven mounts are the pearl divers of Gujarat –

Following the thin and straggling line,
In the steps of Porbandar's grocer,
A movement rooted in dance. The moon marigold
Spinned into the lineage of the weaver, born to Kashmir,
In the year of the coming of the ninth Earl of Elgin,
Over the mills of Bombay, spindling the biography of
A race, held later in one birthcry.

It was a movement rooted in dance.

A white Gucci flannel, a tie bowed gracefully
At the whiff of damoiselles, all manners –
No pretence – the act of the indentured,
Dressed in the habit of the empire, stolid in purpose.
He forgot the taste of his name
In his own tongue.
On breaking out first to the world
On a bullock ride, the journey was haunted
By loneliness, for the shy one, lingering
Flirtingly with the hours.

Crossing the arches, through the partition,
And the cold smog of Karachi,
the swollen eyes of the day,
opened like a bowl of light.

ii.

It was April –
The month that fed me violets.

Time was adolescent in sleeveless clothes,
When the rapturous pilgrim entered the sanctuary,
and found the maiden, kneeling in supplication
at the feet of our lady of mercy, in Cook County,
where the word had gone out earlier,
from the tea leaves, that she would there find,
her dark one. There is mystery there. And a story –
child of the nautilic wind:
each narrative strand kneaded into the dough
of time, and place, becomes the bread of your life,
to be eaten gently. There is history there –

At the eleven cities,
Broken in two, seeping
Out of the inlet of Westergea,
Running from the lake Burgum,
Towards the city of Ljouwert.

From this land the oar sought the waters,
Full was the sail that billowed in the wind
Towards the Bight of Biafra,
Berthing among the coastal reefs, carrying
Its great fevers inland to shore. Among them,
Your kinsman, son of the daughter of Friesland,
And of Mata Hari, from whose distant shores,
Your blood has mingled, in the dance of the ages,
And flowed –

iii.

Like the blood of those too, sent into captivity,
Through the tangled routes,
From the oilbean forests of Umuoma,
To the white beaches of Igweocha, through the
Bowel of the tide, to St. Lucia,
To the windswept marshes of Glyn,
To Dunbar Creek.

You can still see their remnants, child,
At Canon Point's plantation, and hear
Their spirits, wailing, in the marshes, in the
Winds of St. Simon's Island.

The hard wind rocking your pendulum
Back and forth –
Over spumes of bitter waves,
At the place of the Igbo Landing
Where the waters stirred with defiance,
And the freed spirits followed their trail homewards,
Through the sombre aisles of the milky way.
There too, is history.

iv.

For as I turn away from the street
Where its face opened like an old scar
Brooding, the grey crumbling castles
And their lintels from which ancient greed has walked
I think only of the bonded.
Their arched backs still bent by shame.
From Delmar, the Castlereagh,
And the temple of the Masons,
And all the grand evacuated things
I think about how time has undone all things.

I think of the secular, unversed,
Absolute margins, in the architecture of cities,
Built on the indentured backs of men,
And how we have kept our places,
Ephemeral – in this land of migrants.
There is history, my child, where you have nestled.

LAST WILL AND TESTAMENT

Three boxes will contain my will
In a fascicle. It will be all that the
Future will get from me.
A locked box will contain my
Awkward name. My frail identity.
My mind in its ornate complexity,
A second, will hold a locket of hair
From my dashing years.
The third: three poems, one to the unborn,
My swooning words, my eyes that have
Beheld the fever. Some will call it
Psycho – others will analyse it.

But, child, to whom do I leave the unsaid things?
Those unnamable things that still clutch to my throat?
What anger, posted from another century,
Another clime, can smoothen the frown,
From the face of the world?

Kraftgriots

Also in the series (POETRY) *continued*

Ebi Yeibo: *Maiden Lines* (2004)
Barine Ngaage: *Rhythms of Crisis* (2004)
Funso Aiyejina: *I,The Supreme & Other Poems* (2004)
'Lere Oladitan: *Boolekaja: Lagos Poems 1* (2005)
Seyi Adigun: *Bard on the Shore* (2005)
Famous Dakolo: *A Letter to Flora* (2005)
Olawale Durojaiye: *An African Night* (2005)
g'ebinyõ Ogbowei: *let the honey run & other poems* (2005)
Joe Ushie: *Popular Stand & Other Poems* (2005)
Gbemisola Adeoti: *Naked Soles* (2005)
Aj. Dagga Tolar: *This Country is not a Poem* (2005)
Tunde Adeniran: *Labyrinthine Ways* (2006)
Sophia Obi: *Tears in a Basket* (2006)
Tonyo Biriabebe: *Undercurrents* (2006)
Ademola O. Dasylva: *Songs of Odamolugbe* (2006), winner, 2006 ANA/Cadbury poetry prize
George Ehusani: *Flames of Truth* (2006)
Abubakar Gimba: *This Land of Ours* (2006)
g'ebinyõ Ogbowei: *the heedless ballot box* (2006)
Hyginus Ekwuazi: *Love Apart* (2006), winner, 2007 ANA/NDDC Gabriel Okara poetry
     prize and winner, 2007 ANA/Cadbury poetry prize
Abubakar Gimba: *Inner Rumblings* (2006)
Albert Otto: *Letters from the Earth* (2007)
Aj. Dagga Tolar: *Darkwaters Drunkard* (2007)
Idris Okpanachi: *The Eaters of the Living* (2007), winner, 2008 ANA/Cadbury poetry prize
Tubal-Cain: *Mystery in Our Stream* (2007), winner, 2006 ANA/NDDC Gabriel Okara
     poetry prize
John Iwuh: *Ashes & Daydreams* (2007)
Sola Owonibi: *Chants to the Ancestors* (2007)
Adewale Aderinale: *The Authentic* (2007)
Ebi Yeibo: *The Forbidden Tongue* (2007)
Doutimi Kpakiama: *Salute to our Mangrove Giants* (2008)
Halima M. Usman: *Spellbound* (2008)
Hyginus Ekwuazi: *Dawn Into Moonlight: All Around Me Dawning* (2008), winner, 2008
     ANA/NDDC Gabriel Okara poetry prize
Ismail Bala Garba & Abdullahi Ismaila (eds.): *Pyramids: An Anthology of Poems from
     Northern Nigeria* (2008)
Denja Abdullahi: *Abuja Nunyi (This is Abuja)* (2008)
Japhet Adeneye: *Poems for Teenagers* (2008)
Seyi Hodonu: *A Tale of Two in Time (Letters to Susan)* (2008)
Ibukun Babarinde: *Running Splash of Rust and Gold* (2008)
Chris Ngozi Nkoro: *Trails of a Distance* (2008)
Tunde Adeniran: *Beyond Finalities* (2008)
Abba Abdulkareem: *A Bard's Balderdash* (2008)

Ifeanyi D. Ogbonnaya: ... *And Pigs Shall Become House Cleaners* (2008)
g'ebinyŏ ogbowei: *the town crier's song* (2009)
g'ebinyŏ ogbowei: *song of a dying river* (2009)
Sophia Obi-Apoko: *Floating Snags* (2009)
Akachi Adimora-Ezeigbo: *Heart Songs* (2009), winner, 2009 ANA/Cadbury poetry prize
Hyginus Ekwuazi: *The Monkey's Eyes* (2009)
Seyi Adigun: *Prayer for the Mwalimu* (2009)
Faith A. Brown: *Endless Season* (2009)
B.M. Dzukogi: *Midnight Lamp* (2009)
B.M. Dzukogi: *These Last Tears* (2009)
Chimezie Ezechukwu: *The Nightingale* (2009)
Ummi Kaltume Abdullahi: *Tiny Fingers* (2009)
Ismaila Bala & Ahmed Maiwada (eds.): *Fireflies: An Anthology of New Nigerian Poetry* (2009)
Eugenia Abu: *Don't Look at Me Like That* (2009)
Data Osa Don-Pedro: *You Are Gold and Other Poems* (2009)
Sam Omatseye: *Mandela's Bones and Other Poems* (2009)
Sam Omatseye: *Dear Baby Ramatu* (2009)
C.O. Iyimoga: *Fragments in the Air* (2010)
Bose Ayeni-Tsevende: *Streams* (2010)
Seyi Hodonu: *Songs from My Mother's Heart (2010),* winner ANA/NDDC Gabriel Okara
    poetry prize, 2010
Akachi Adimora-Ezeigbo: *Waiting for Dawn* (2010)
Hyginus Ekwuazi: *That Other Country* (2010), winner, ANA/Cadbury poetry prize, 2010
Emmanuel Frank-Opigo: *Masks and Facades* (2010)
Tosin Otitoju: *Comrade* (2010)
Arnold Udoka: *Poems Across Borders* (2010)
Arnold Udoka: *The Gods Are So Silent & Other Poems* (2010)
Abubakar Othman: *The Passions of Cupid* (2010)
Okinba Launko: *Dream-Seeker on Divining Chain* (2010)
'kufre ekanem: *the ant eaters* (2010)
McNezer Fasehun: *Ever Had a Dear Sister* (2010)
Baba S. Umar: *A Portrait of My People* (2010)
Gimba Kakanda: *Safari Pants* (2010)
Sam Omatseye: *Lion Wind & Other Poems* (2011)
Ify Omalicha: *Now that Dreams are Born* (2011)
Karo Okokoh: *Souls of a Troubadour* (2011)
Ada Onyebuenyi, Chris Ngozi Nkoro, Ebere Chukwu (eds): *Uto Nka: An Anthology of
    Literature for Fresh Voices* (2011)
Mabel Osakwe: *Desert Songs of Bloom* (2011)
Pious Okoro: *Vultures of Fortune & Other Poems* (2011)
Godwin Yina: *Clouds of Sorrows* (2011)
Nnimmo Bassey: *I Will Not Dance to Your Beat* (2011)
Denja Abdullahi: *A Thousand Years of Thirst* (2011)
Enoch Ojotisa: *Commoner's Speech* (2011)
Rowland Timi Kpakiama: *Bees and Beetles* (2011)
Niyi Osundare: *Random Blues* (2011)
Lawrence Ogbo Ugwuanyi: *Let Them Not Run* (2011)

Saddiq M. Dzukogi: *Canvas* (2011

Arnold Udoka: *Running with My Rivers* (2011)

Olusanya Bamidele: *Erased Without a Trace* (2011)

Olufolake Jegede: *Treasure Pods* (2012)

Karo Okokoh: *Songs of a Griot* (2012), winner. ANA/NDDC Gabriel Okara poetry prize, 2012

Musa Idris Okpanachi: *From the Margins of Paradise* (2012)

John Martins Agba: *The Fiend and Other Poems* (2012)

Sunnie Ododo: *Broken Pitchers* (2012)

'Kunmi Adeoti: *Epileptic City* (2012)

Ibiwari Ikiriko: *Oily Tears of the Delta* (2012)

Bala Dalhatu: *Moonlights* (2012)

Karo Okokoh: *Manna for the Mind* (2012)

Chika O. Agbo: *The Fury of the Gods* (2012)

Emmanuel C. S. Ojukwu: *Beneath the Sagging Roof* (2012)

Amirikpa Oyigbenu: *Cascades and Flakes* (2012)

Ebi Yeibo: *Shadows of the Setting Sun* (2012)

Chikaoha Agoha: *Shreds of Thunder* (2012)

Mark Okorie: *Terror Verses* (2012)

Clemmy Igwebike-Ossi: *Daisies in the Desert* (2012)

Idris Amali: *Back Again (At the Foothills of Greed)* (2012)

A.N. Akwanya: *Visitant on Tiptoe* (2012)

Akachi Adimora-Ezeigbo: *Dancing Masks* (2013)

Chinazo-Bertrand Okeomah: *Furnace of Passion* (2013)

g'ebinyŏ ogbowei: *marsh boy and other poems* (2013)

Ifeoma Chinwuba: *African Romance* (2013)

Remi Raji: *Sea of my Mind* (2013)

Francis Odinya: *Never Cry Again in Babylon* (2013)

Immanuel Unekwuojo Ogu: *Musings of a Pilgrim* (2013)

Khabyr Fasasi: *Tongues of Warning* (2013)

J.C.P. Christopher: *Salient Whispers* (2014)

Paul T. Liam: *Saint Sha'ade and other poems* (2014)

Joy Nwiyi: *Burning Bottom* (2014)

R. Adebayo Lawal: *Melodreams* (2014)

R. Adebayo Lawal: *Music of the Muezzin* (2014)

Idris Amali: *Efeega: War of Ants* (2014)

Samuel Onungwe: *Tantrums of a King* (2014)

Bizuum G. Yadok: *Echoes of the Plateau* (2014)

Abubakar Othman: *Bloodstreams in the Desert* (2014)

rome aboh: *A Torrent of Terror* (2014)

Udenta O. Udenta: *37 Seasons Before the Tornado* (2015)

Magnus Abraham-Dukuma: *Dreams from the Creek* (2015)

Christian Otobotekere: *A Sailor's Son* (2015)

Tanure Ojaide: *The Tale of the Harmattan* (2015)

Festus Okwekwe: *Our Mother is Not a Woman* (2015)

Tunde Adeniran: *Fate and Faith* (2015)

Khabyr Fasasi: *Spells of Solemn Songs* (2015)

Chris Anyokwu: *Naked Truth* (2015)

Zoya Jibodu: *Melodies of Love* (2015)
Tanure Ojaide: *Songs of Myself: Quartet* (2015)
Rita Nsiegbe: *Pool of Love* (2016)
Abdul-Rasheed Na'Allah: *Obama Mentum* (2016)
Toyin Shittu: *Naija Blues and Other Poems* (2016)

Printed in the United States
By Bookmasters